SEA OTTERS

ASHLEY GISH

MARINE X MAMMALS

ARCTIC
OCEAN

ATLANTIC
OCEAN

PACIFIC
OCEAN

INDIAN
OCEAN

SOUTHERN
OCEAN

CREATIVE EDUCATION · CREATIVE PAPERBACKS

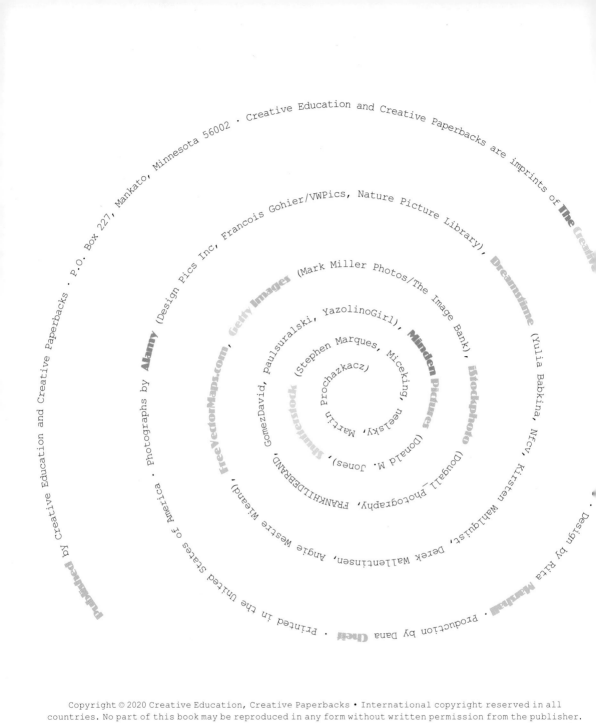

Published by Creative Education and Creative Paperbacks · P.O. Box 227, Mankato, Minnesota 56002 · Creative Education and Creative Paperbacks are imprints of The Creative Company · www.thecreativecompany.us · Design by Rita Marshall · Production by Dana Cheit · Printed in the United States of America · Photographs by Alamy (Design Pics Inc, Francois Gohier/VWPics, Nature Picture Library), Dreamstime (Yulia Babkina, Nfcv, Kirsten Wahlquist, Derek Wallentinsen, Angie Westre Wieand), FreeVectorMaps.com, Getty Images (Mark Miller Photos/The Image Bank), iStockphoto (Donald_Photography, FRANKHILDEBRAND, GomezDavid, paulsuralski, YazolinoGirl), Minden Pictures (Stephen Marques, Miceking, neelsky, Donald M. Jones), Shutterstock (Martin Prochazkacz)

Copyright © 2020 Creative Education, Creative Paperbacks • International copyright reserved in all countries. No part of this book may be reproduced in any form without written permission from the publisher. Library of Congress Cataloging-in-Publication Data • Names: Gish, Ashley, author. • Title: Sea otters / Ashley Gish. • Series: X-Books: Marine mammals. • Includes index. • Summary: A countdown of five of the most captivating sea otters provides thrills as readers learn about the biological, social, and hunting characteristics of intelligent marine mammals. • Identifiers: LCCN: 2018048286 / ISBN 978-1-64026-192-1 (hardcover) / ISBN 978-1-62832-755-7 (pbk) / ISBN 978-1-64000-310-1 (eBook) • Subjects: LCSH: 1. Sea otter—Behavior—Juvenile literature. 2. Sea otter—Juvenile literature. • Classification: LCC QL737.C25 G576 2019 / DDC 599.769/5—dc23 • CCSS: RI.3.1-8; RI.4.1-5, 7; RI.5.1-3, 8; RI.6.1-2, 4, 7; RH.6-8.3-8
First Edition HC 9 8 7 6 5 4 3 2 1 • First Edition PBK 9 8 7 6 5 4 3 2 1

SEA OTTERS

CONTENTS

MARINE X MAMMALS

XCEPTIONAL MARINE MAMMALS

Sea otters are cute. They have thick fur and muscular tails. They are also very smart. They have impressive survival skills. They are one of the few animals that use tools to get to their food.

Sea Otter Basics

Sea otters are related to weasels and badgers. They are among are the biggest members of the weasel family. But they are the smallest **marine mammals**. Sea otters spend most of their lives in the ocean. They float on kelp forests. Kelp is a kind of seaweed. It grows up from the ocean floor. The top of a kelp forest is the canopy. Sea otters can survive in places where kelp does not grow. But they prefer to live in kelp forests. They are comfortable and safe in the canopy.

ASIA

sea otter range

PACIFIC
OCEAN

NORTHERN PACIFIC

Asian, northern, and southern sea otters
all live in the northern Pacific Ocean. They are
typically seen within a few miles of shore.

MALE SEA OTTERS

Male sea otters weigh 60 to
90 pounds (27.2–40.8 kg). They measure
about five feet (1.5 m) in length.

FEMALE SEA OTTERS

Female sea otters weigh 35 to 60 pounds (15.9–27.2 kg). They are between three and four and a half feet (0.9–1.4 m) long.

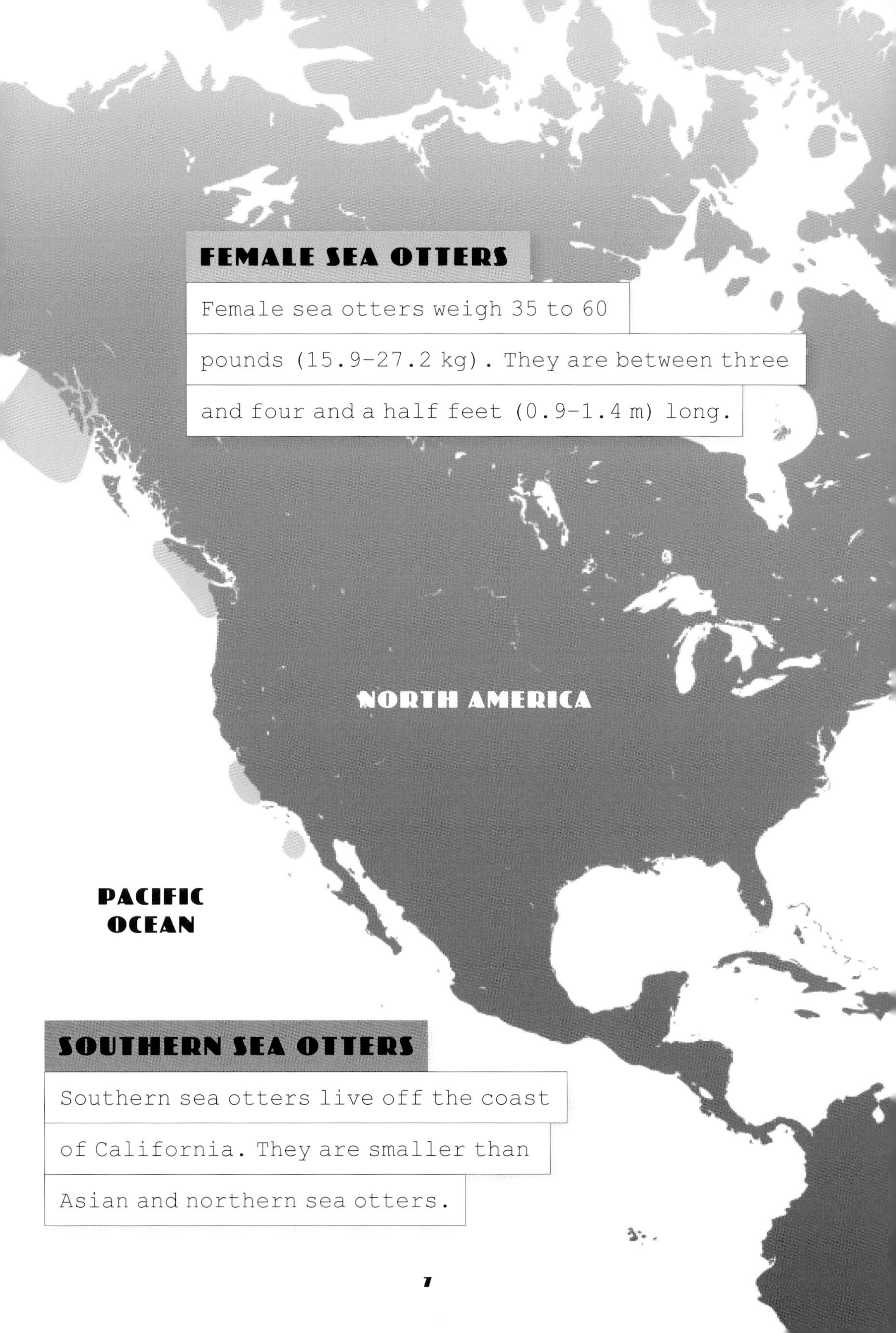

NORTH AMERICA

PACIFIC
OCEAN

SOUTHERN SEA OTTERS

Southern sea otters live off the coast of California. They are smaller than Asian and northern sea otters.

Sea otters eat shellfish and **crustaceans**.

They have powerful front paws.

If they cannot pry open a shell, they

will smash it. A sea otter keeps a rock

tucked in the loose skin under its armpit.

SMASHING
SHELLS

Sea otters are suited to life in the water. They have
long, thick tails. Their large hind feet are **webbed**.
Tucking in their small forepaws, they use their tail
and hind feet to swim. Unlike other marine mammals,
sea otters do not have a thick layer of fat. Instead,
their dense fur keeps them warm. They have two layers
of fur. The top layer is waterproof. The bottom layer
traps warm air. This also helps sea otters stay afloat.

Sea otters spend hours grooming daily.

KEEPING CLEAN

SEA OTTER BASICS FACT

Sea otters range in color from light brown to black.

Their paws and faces get lighter as they age.

TOP FIVE XTREME SEA OTTERS

Xtreme Sea Otter #5

Famous Foster Mom In 2001, the Monterey Bay Aquarium rescued a sea otter. She was sick. She would not have survived in the wild. The southern sea otter was named Toola. She went on to raise 13 orphaned sea otter pups. Eleven of them were released into the wild. Toola helped introduce a law in 2006. It protects wild sea otters. It also supports research into diseases and other threats. Toola died in 2012.

Sea otters need to eat about 25 percent

of their body weight every day.

Sea Otter Babies

Sea otter babies are called pups. A mother gives birth to a single pup. Pups are born in the water. The newborns weigh three to five pounds (1.4–2.3 kg). They are completely helpless. They rely on their mothers for food and protection for about six months.

Mothers carry their pups on their bellies. Pups drink milk from their mother for six to eight months. Mothers teach pups how to swim and hunt soon after birth. Pups learn how to open hard shells with rocks. They learn how to eat a crab without getting pinched.

Much of a mother's time is spent grooming her pup. Pups are born with woolly fur. It helps them float. They cannot dive underwater until they shed this coat, around two or three months of age. If a mother sea otter senses danger, she will grab her pup's neck with her teeth. Then she dives underwater, pulling the pup to safety.

at birth

4
pounds
(1.8 kg)

6
weeks

Pup is born

Eats solid foods

Swims

1
month

2 to **3** months

Begins diving

3 months

Learns to hunt

4 years females

Reproduces

6 years males

SEA OTTER BABIES FACT

Pups make high-pitched squeals to get their mothers' attention.

Mothers and their pups recognize each other's voices.

Xtreme Sea Otter #4

A Promising Comeback Before 1740, there were roughly 300,000 sea otters worldwide. But fur traders loved sea otter fur. The animals were hunted relentlessly. By 1911, there were only about 2,000 sea otters left. People thought southern sea otters had died out completely. But a small group was discovered in 1938. Since then, the southern sea otter's numbers have slowly increased. In 2016, there were an estimated 3,000 southern sea otters in California.

Most of the time, sea otters are quiet.

Happy sea otters make grunting or cooing sounds.

100% of sea otters

10%

90%

live in other areas

live in Alaska

XTRAORDINARY LIFESTYLE

Sea otters can go their entire lives without stepping foot on land. They often rest in groups called rafts. A raft may have anywhere from 2 to 2,000 sea otters!

Their whiskers help them find food.

Sea Otter Society

Northern sea otters form the largest rafts around Alaska. Southern and Asian sea otters are less social. Males form rafts separately from females and pups. When an unfamiliar sea otter approaches a raft, its members touch him with their noses. They jerk their heads from side to side. This helps them smell the newcomer. They will remember his scent next time he passes through.

Some male sea otters establish territories. They chase away other males. Females can move freely between male territories. Male sea otters will attempt to mate with females that enter their territory. When mating, males become aggressive with females. A male will bite his mate's nose and spin her around. Up to 10 percent of female sea otters drown during mating.

XEMPLARY SKILLS FACT

Sea otters close their nostrils and ears while diving.

Dives typically last less than three minutes.

XEMPLARY SKILLS

Sea otters are not fast swimmers. Underwater, they swim less than six miles (9.7 km) per hour. But they are effective foragers. Nearly 85 percent of sea otter dives for food are successful.

While sleeping, sea otters sometimes hold each other's paws. This keeps them close together through the night.

Sea otters dive to the ocean floor. There they hunt shellfish and crustaceans. The deepest recorded sea otter dive was more than 325 feet (99.1 m). But they rarely dive deeper than 100 feet (30.5 m). Sea otters help control sea urchin populations. This benefits kelp forests. Kelp, in turn, helps sea otters. Sea otters spend most of their time floating on their backs. They wrap themselves in kelp. This keeps them from drifting away while they rest.

Sea otters have **retractable** claws on their front paws. These are useful for grooming and capturing food. Sea otters store a rock in their underarm pocket. They tuck food there, too. When they surface after foraging, they set their rock on their chest. Then they pound their hard-shelled meal against it. This breaks the creature's shell.

3

TOP FIVE XTREME SEA OTTERS

★ Xtreme Sea Otter #3

YouTube Famous One of the most popular videos on YouTube in 2007 featured a pair of sea otters. They held paws while sleeping—just like wild sea otters! The sea otters were named Nyac and Milo. They lived at the Vancouver Aquarium. Nyac, a female, was rescued after the 1989 *Exxon Valdez* oil spill in Alaska. Milo, a male, was born at an aquarium in Portugal in 1999.

again at risk of dying out. They are threatened by human actions. Their numbers have been decreasing steadily for the last 50 years.

Sea Otter Survival

Pollution causes many problems for sea otters. Oil spills are often caused by accidents. In these events, oil flows into the ocean. It floats on top of the water. It sticks to everything it touches. Sea otters cannot clean oil from their fur. The fur loses its warming capability. Sea otters freeze. Even a small amount of oil can cause major problems.

Fishing equipment can trap sea otters. They get tangled in nets and ropes. Then they cannot move. They might drown or starve. Chemicals from factories run into rivers. This polluted water flows into oceans. It can make animals sick. Carefully controlling oil, chemicals, and fishing gear can help keep sea otters safe.

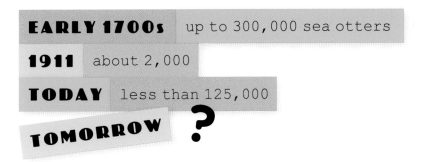

EARLY 1700s up to 300,000 sea otters

1911 about 2,000

TODAY less than 125,000

TOMORROW **?**

But orcas occasionally hunt sea otters. Great white sharks also pose a threat. And eagles are known to snatch up sea otter pups. Sea otters are also threatened by diseases. But most of the dangers they face are from people.

Sea otters are generally safe from predators.

Sea otter numbers have shrunk to half of what they were 50 years ago.

TOP FIVE XTREME SEA OTTERS

Xtreme Sea Otter #2

An Oregon Orphan Monterey Bay
Aquarium rescued a southern sea otter
pup in 2017. He was less than two weeks
old. He had been stranded in California.
Rescuers could not find a female to raise
him. That meant the pup could not go back
into the wild. The Oregon Zoo adopted
him. His care team named him Lincoln. The
zoo uses Lincoln to teach visitors about
the importance of otter conservation.

In the wild, male sea otters live for 10 to 15 years. Females may live up to 20 years.

Sea otters can have one million hairs per square inch (6.5 sq cm) of fur

The hunting of sea otters ended with the 1911 signing of the International Fur Seal Treaty.

Some estimates suggest that only about 25 percent of sea otter pups survive their first year.

In Alaska, most sea otter pups are born in late spring or early summer

Male sea otters choose territories based on abundance of food, kelp, and females.

A 75-pound (34-kg) sea otter can eat up to 1,500 sea urchins in one day

Given a choice between a big abalone and a small one, sea otters choose the bigger one.

If the weather is good, sea otters will mate and give birth more than once in a year.

When frightened, sea otters may hiss, whistle, or scream.

Sea otters are diurnal. They are active during the day and sleep at nigh

Nearly 4,000 sea otters were killed by the 1989 *Exxon Valdez* oil spill.

Before leaving to hunt, sea otter moms wrap their pups in kelp to hold them in place.

Northern sea otters are the most widespread. They range from

Alaska's Aleutian Islands to Washington's Olympic Peninsula.

Xtreme Sea Otter #1

Otter Crossing About 100 sea otters live at Moss Landing, California. Sometimes they travel over land to nearby Elkhorn Slough. In 2015, tragedy struck. A sea otter named Mr. Enchilada was hit and killed by a car on his way to the slough. This spurred changes. Public works crews put in signs and a speed bump. They even made a specially marked sea otter crosswalk. Sea otters actually use it! They safely cross the road.

GLOSSARY

crustaceans – animals that have a hard shell and live in water

grooming – cleaning the fur and skin

marine mammals – animals with a backbone and fur or hair that live in or near the ocean and feed their babies milk

retractable – able to be drawn back or in

webbed – connected by a web of skin

RESOURCES

"Marine Mammals: Sea Otter." Kids Do Ecology. http://kids.nceas.ucsb.edu/mmp/seaotter.html.

Newman, Patricia. *Sea Otter Heroes: The Predators That Saved an Ecosystem*. Minneapolis: Millbrook Press, 2017.

"Sea Otter." National Geographic Kids. https://kids.nationalgeographic.com/animals/sea-otter/.

Spilsbury, Louise. *Sea Otters*. Chicago: Capstone Heinemann Library, 2013.

INDEX

If a sea otter becomes tangled in a net,

others will gather around and try to free it.